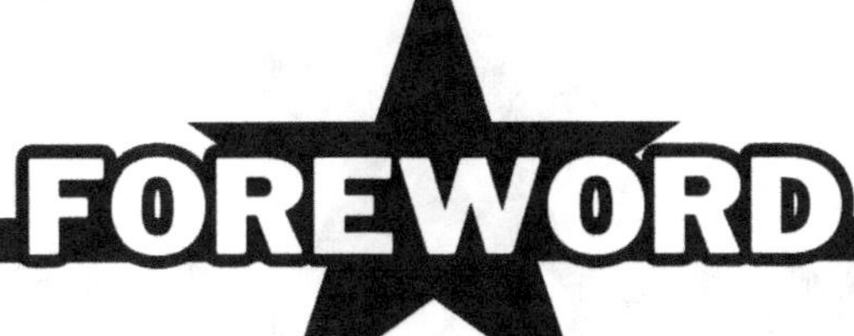

FOREWORD

By the first Black woman to be elected President of the American Institute of Architects (AIA):

"Grab your imagination and your suitcase!
We are going on an exciting journey through the dynamic world of architecture! This delightful coloring book offers page after page of iconic structures from across the globe for you to discover and celebrate.
Let's unleash your creativity and explore some of the great work that architects have been designing throughout history.
Once you finish coloring each page,
you will feel inspired and empowered to create even more.
Like an architect, you can dream up a new design of your own when you get to page 'Y' in this alphabet-organized passport around the world."

- Kimberly Dowdell, AIA

HERE'S YOUR PASSPORT AROUND THE WORLD!

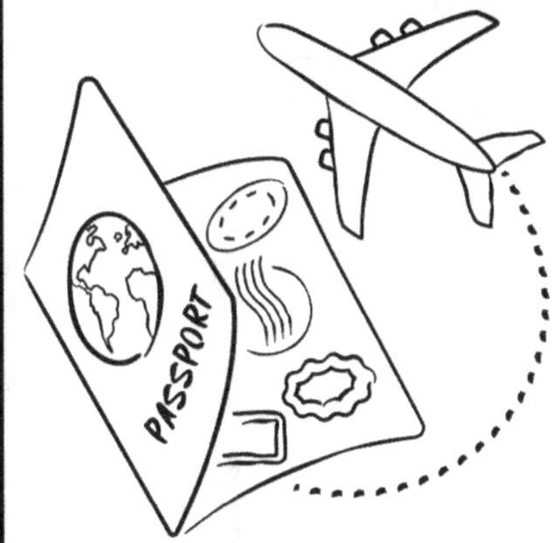

Name:

____

Birthday:

____

I0833868

Place of Birth:

____

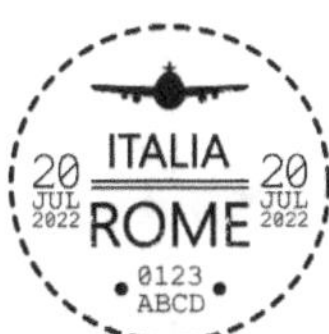

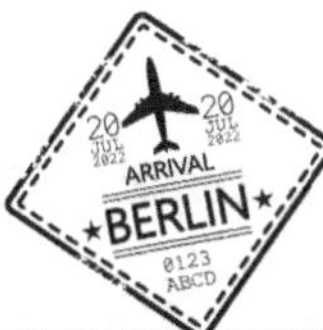

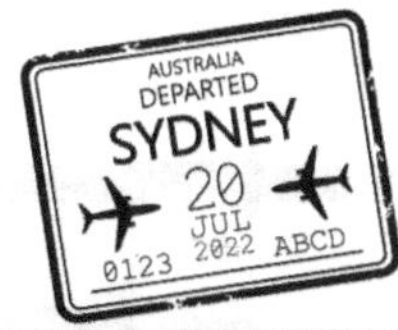

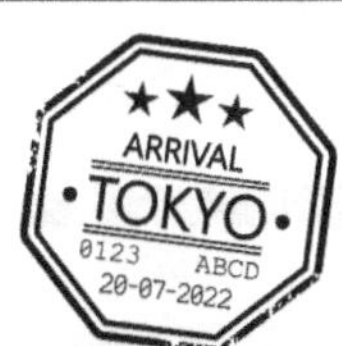

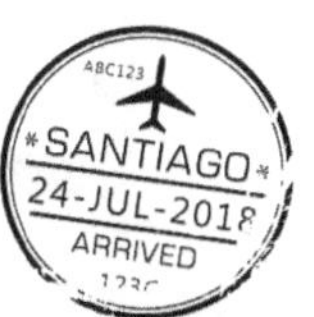

Let's get started! Enjoy!

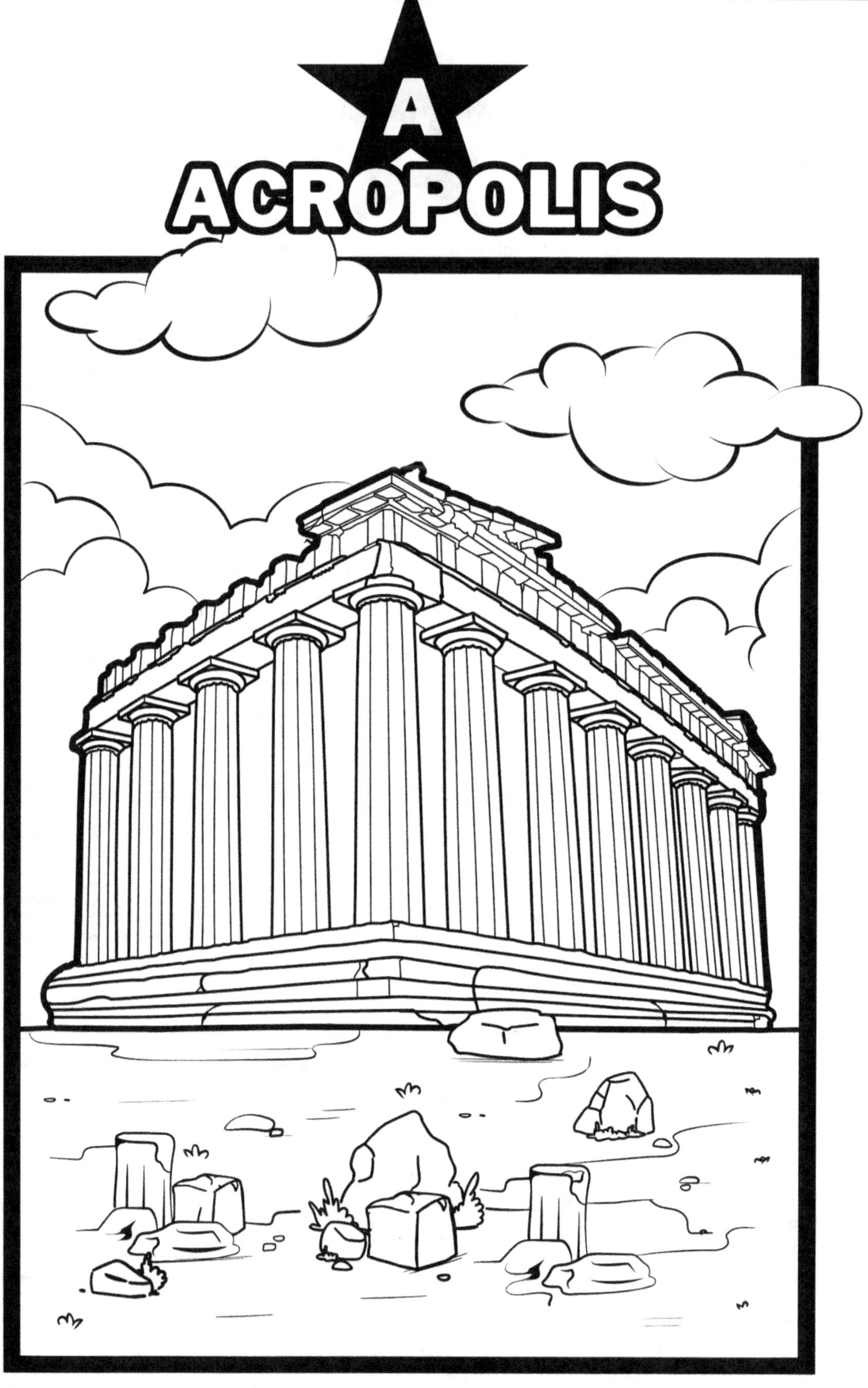

The Acropolis is an ancient mythical home of the gods and a tourist attraction located in Athens, Greece. The Acropolis was designed by Callicrates and Ictinus in the 5th century.

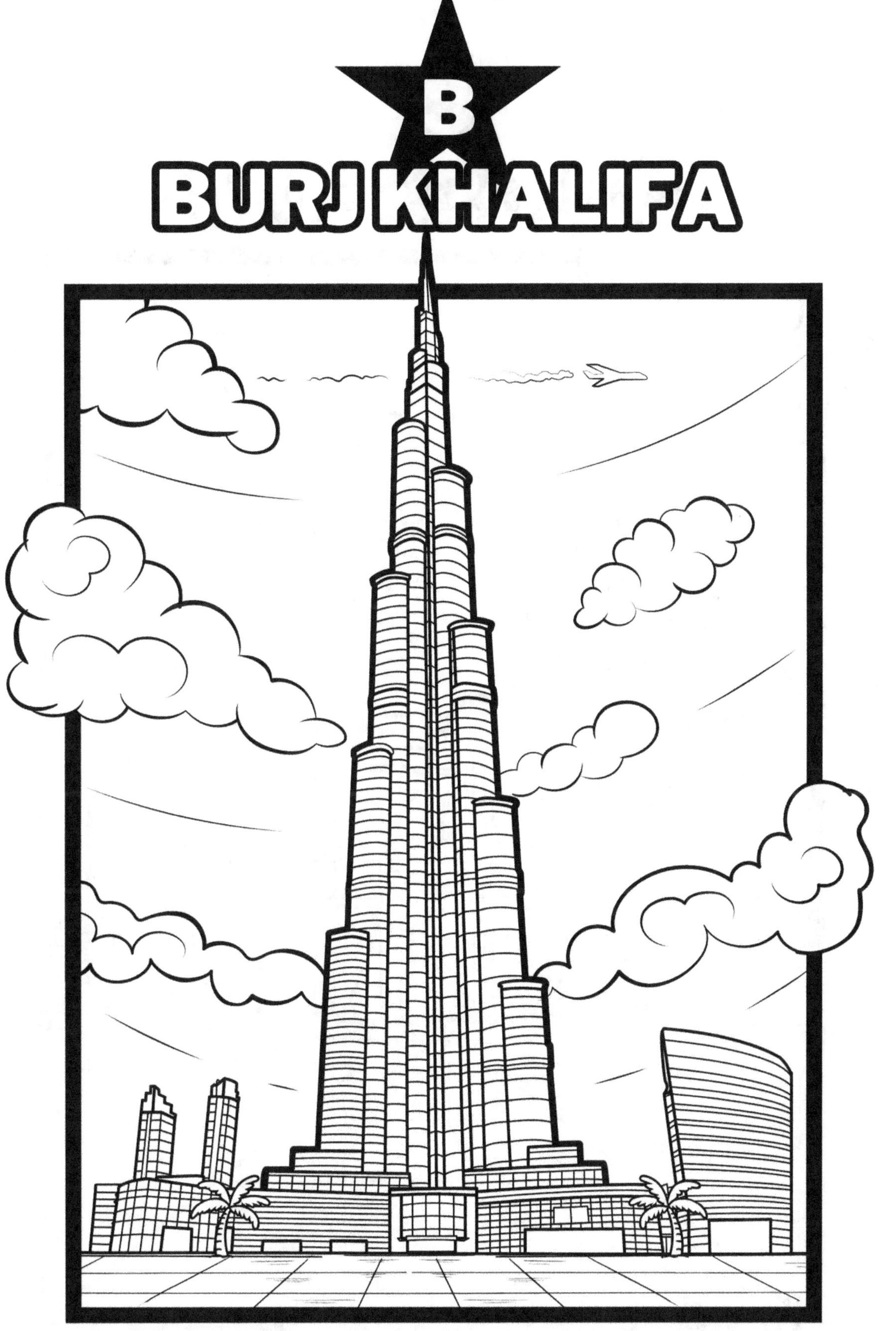

Burj Khalifa is the tallest building in the world.
Burj Khalifa is located in Dubai, United Arab Emirates
and was designed by Adrian Smith and completed in 2010.

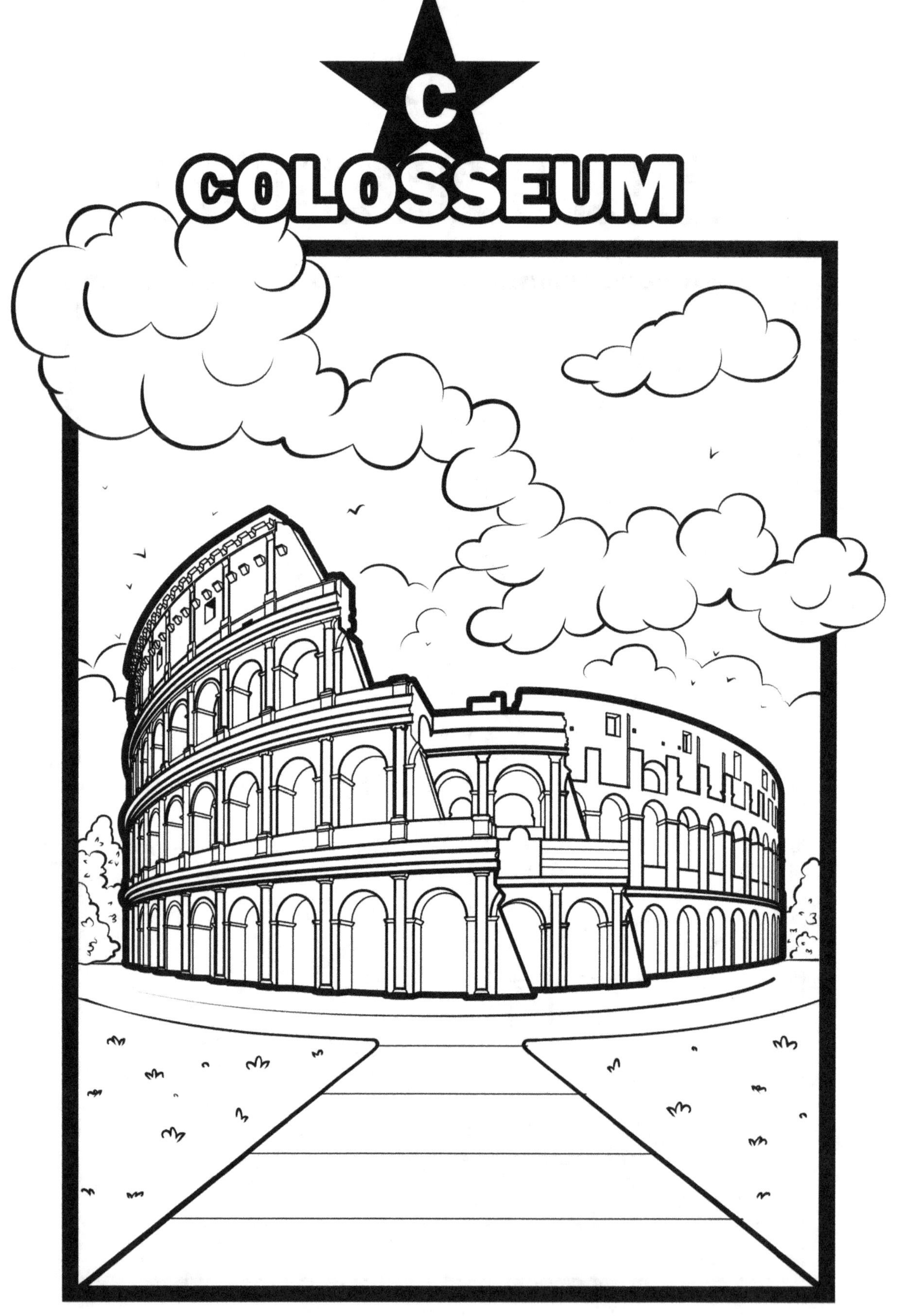

The Colosseum, located in the center of Rome, Italy, is the largest ancient amphitheater ever built. The Colosseum was designed by Vespasian and was completed in AD 80 under his successor and heir, Titus.

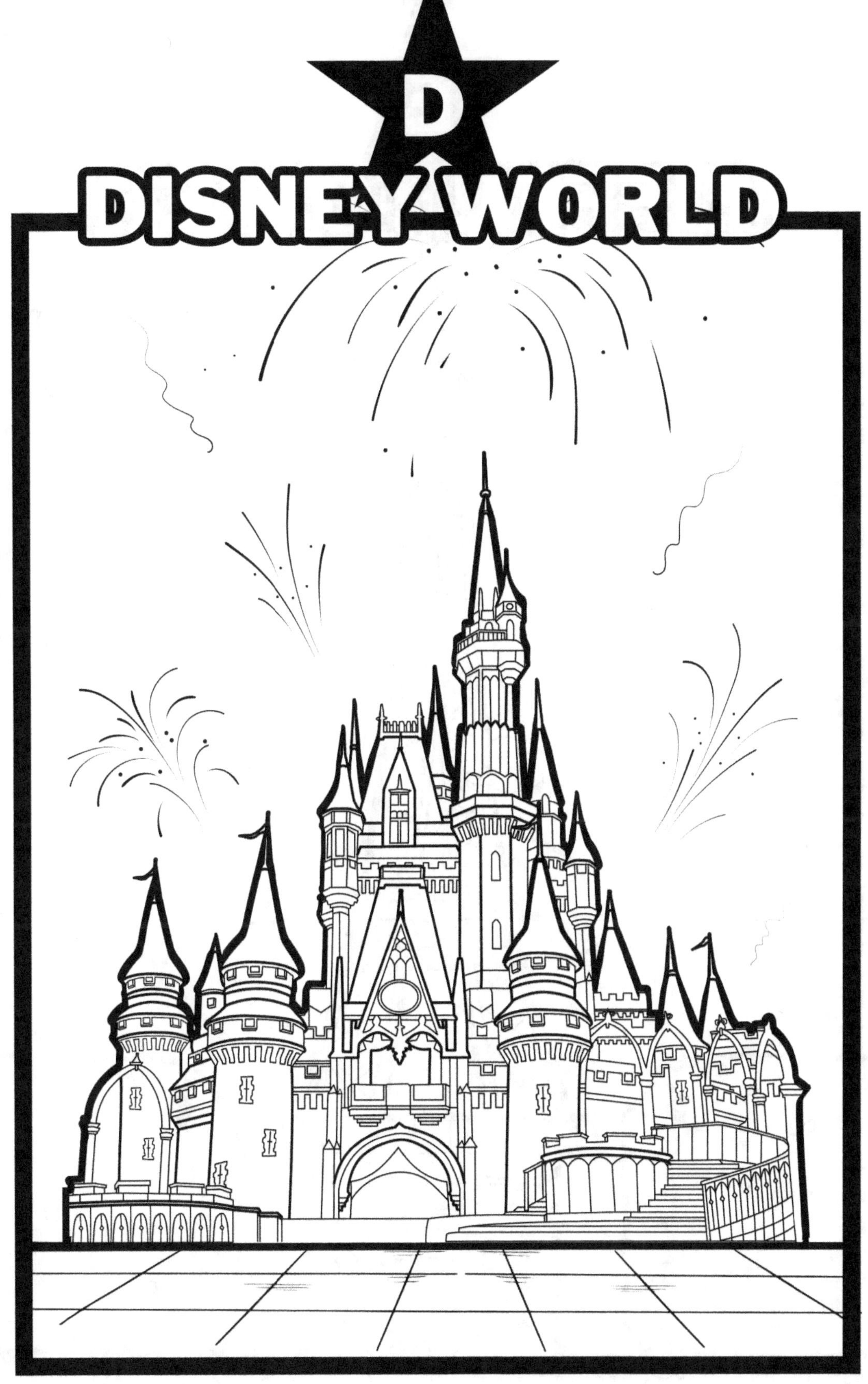

The Walt Disney World® Resort is an entertainment resort in Florida in the United States. The Cinderella Castle at Magic Kingdom in Walt Disney World®, Florida, was designed by imagineer® Herbert Ryman in 1971.

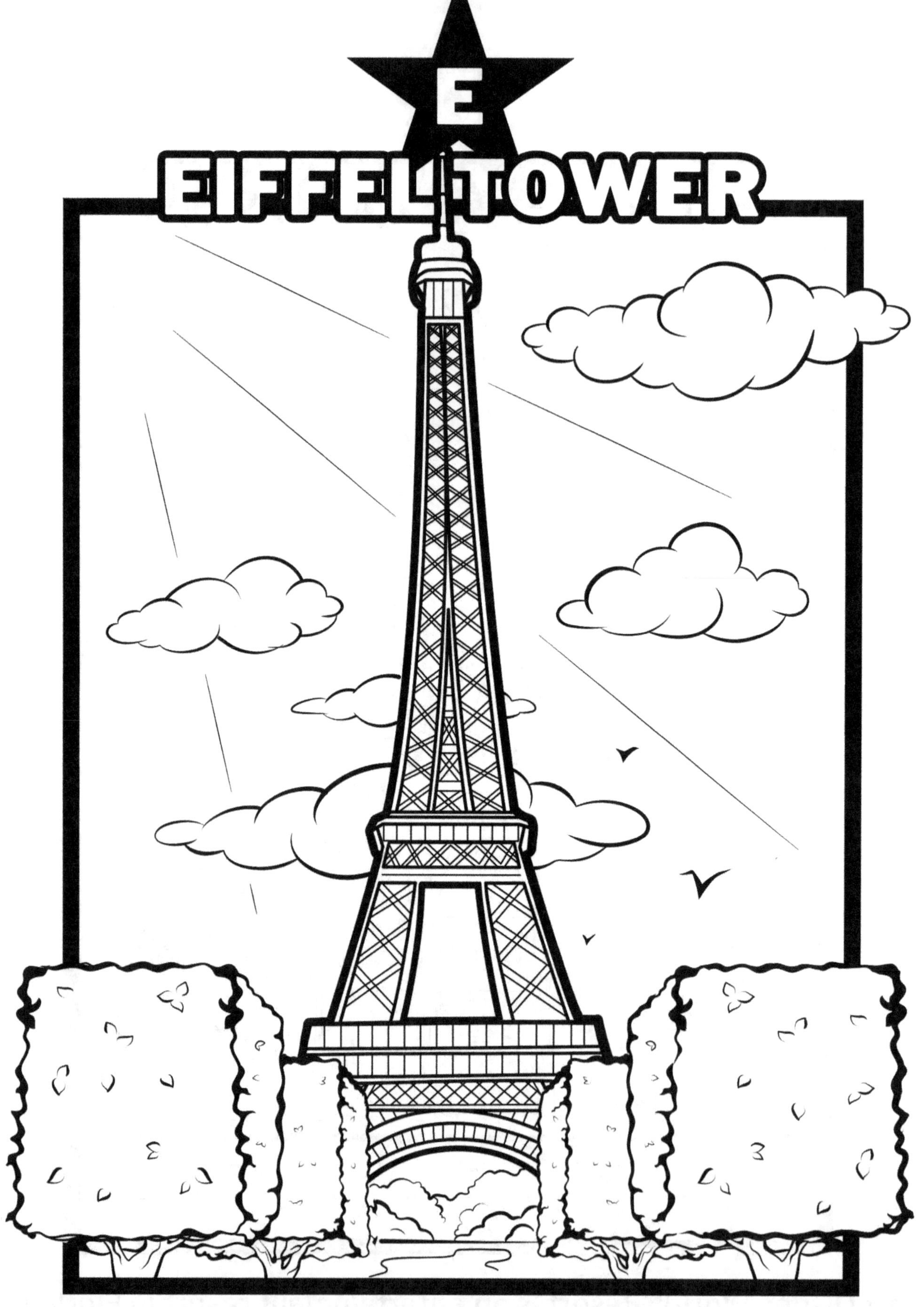

The Eiffel Tower is an iron lattice tower in Paris, France. It is the tallest building in France and is named after the engineer Gustave Eiffel. Construction was completed in 1889.

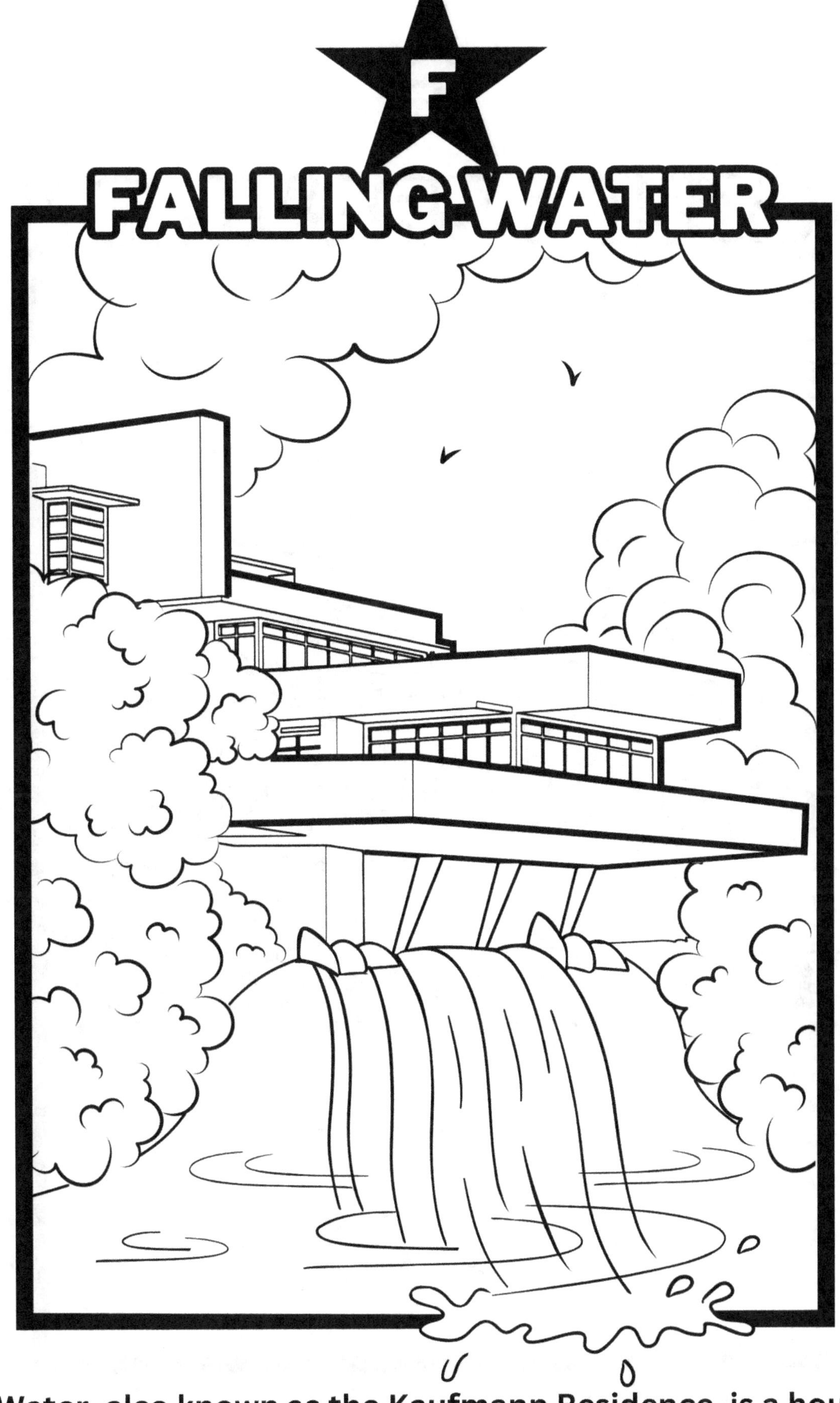

Falling Water, also known as the Kaufmann Residence, is a house in the Laurel Highlands of Pennsylvania in the United States of America. Falling Water was designed by architect Frank Lloyd Wright in 1935.

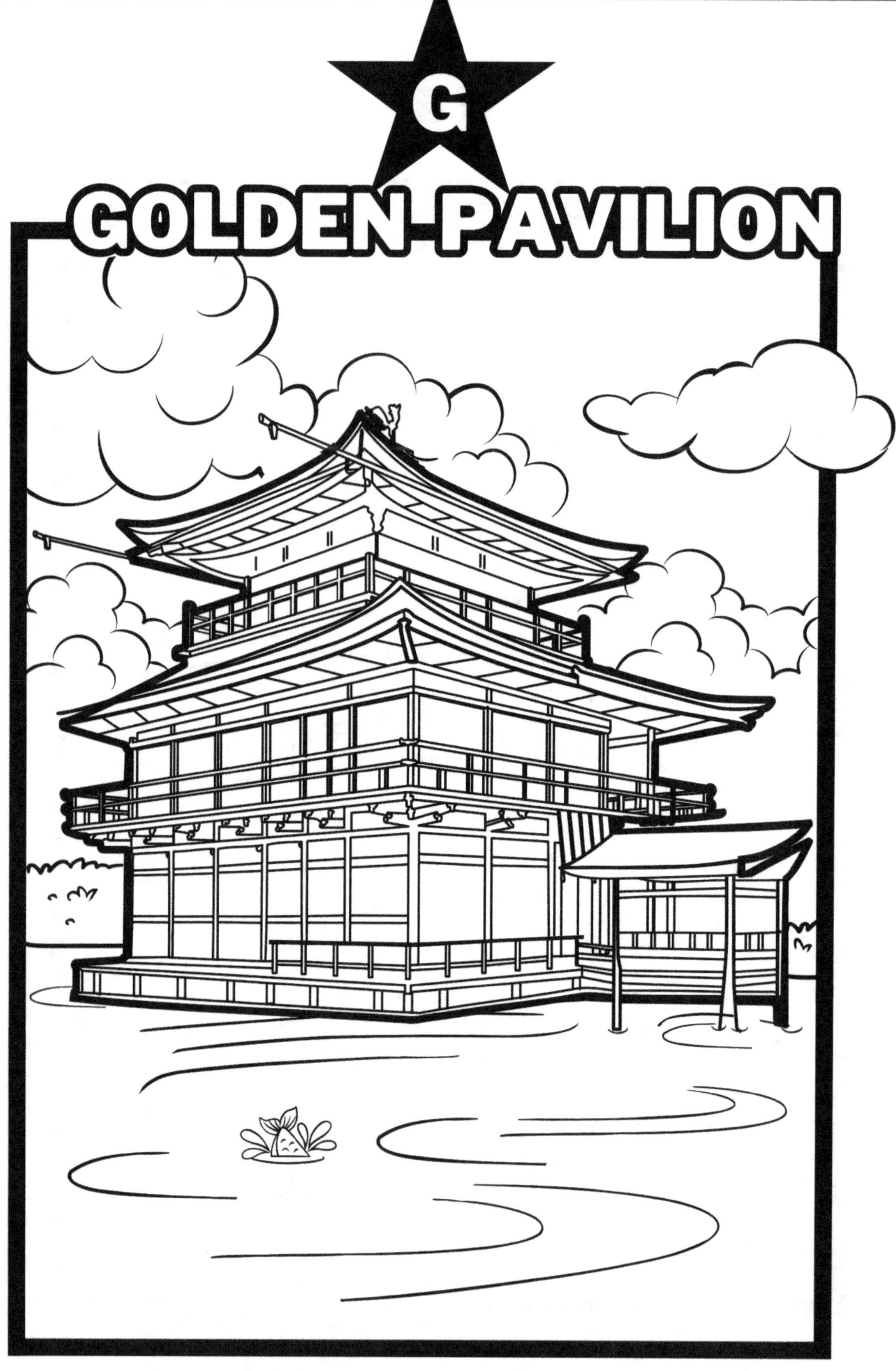

The Golden Pavilion is a Zen Buddhist temple located in Kyoto, Japan.
The temple's top two floors are covered in pure gold leaf.
Ashikaga Yoshimitsu built the temple in 1338 as his retirement villa.

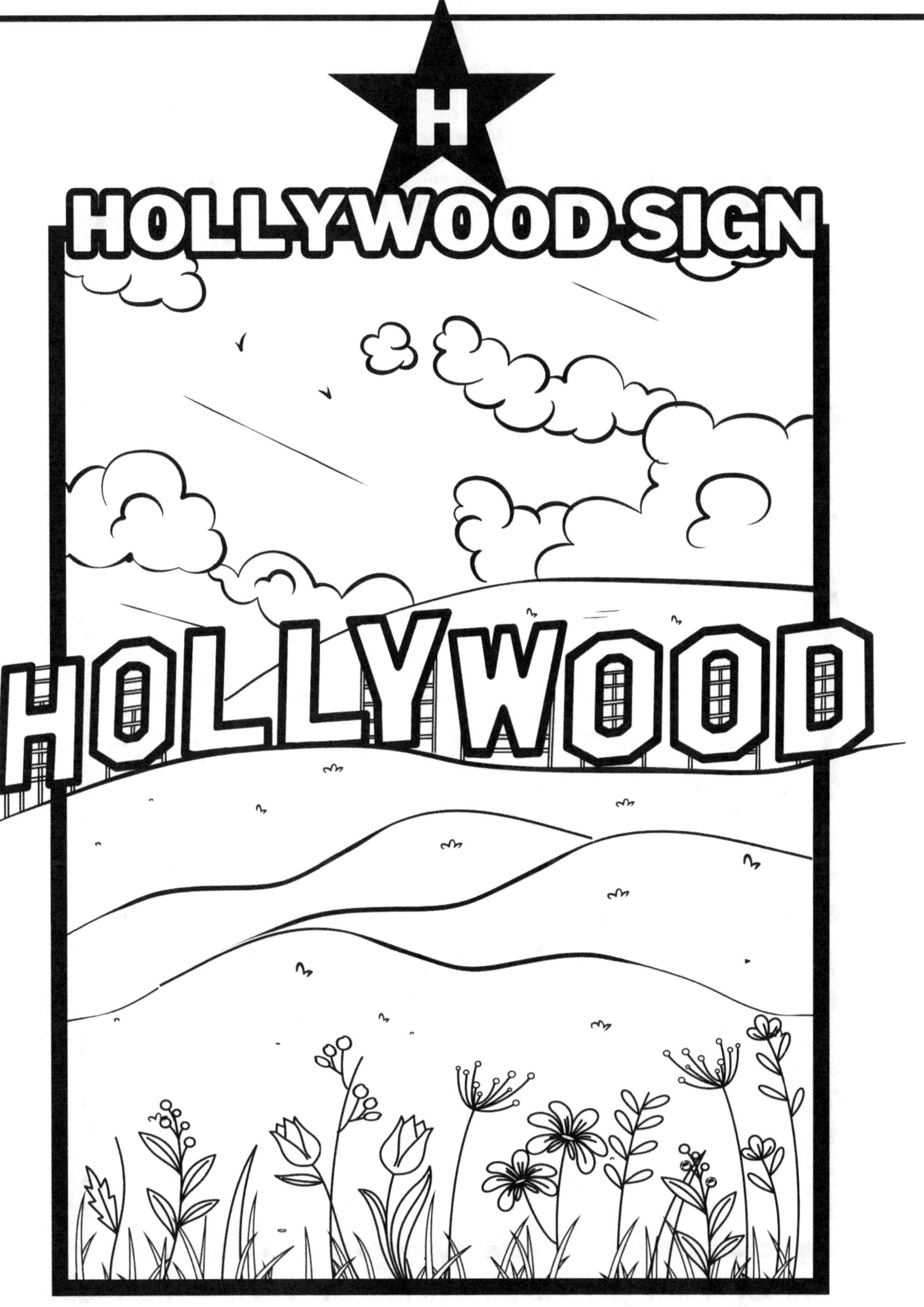

The Hollywood Sign is an American landmark and cultural icon overlooking Hollywood, Los Angeles, California. Thomas Goff designed the sign in 30-foot wide and 50-foot high white block letters in 1923.

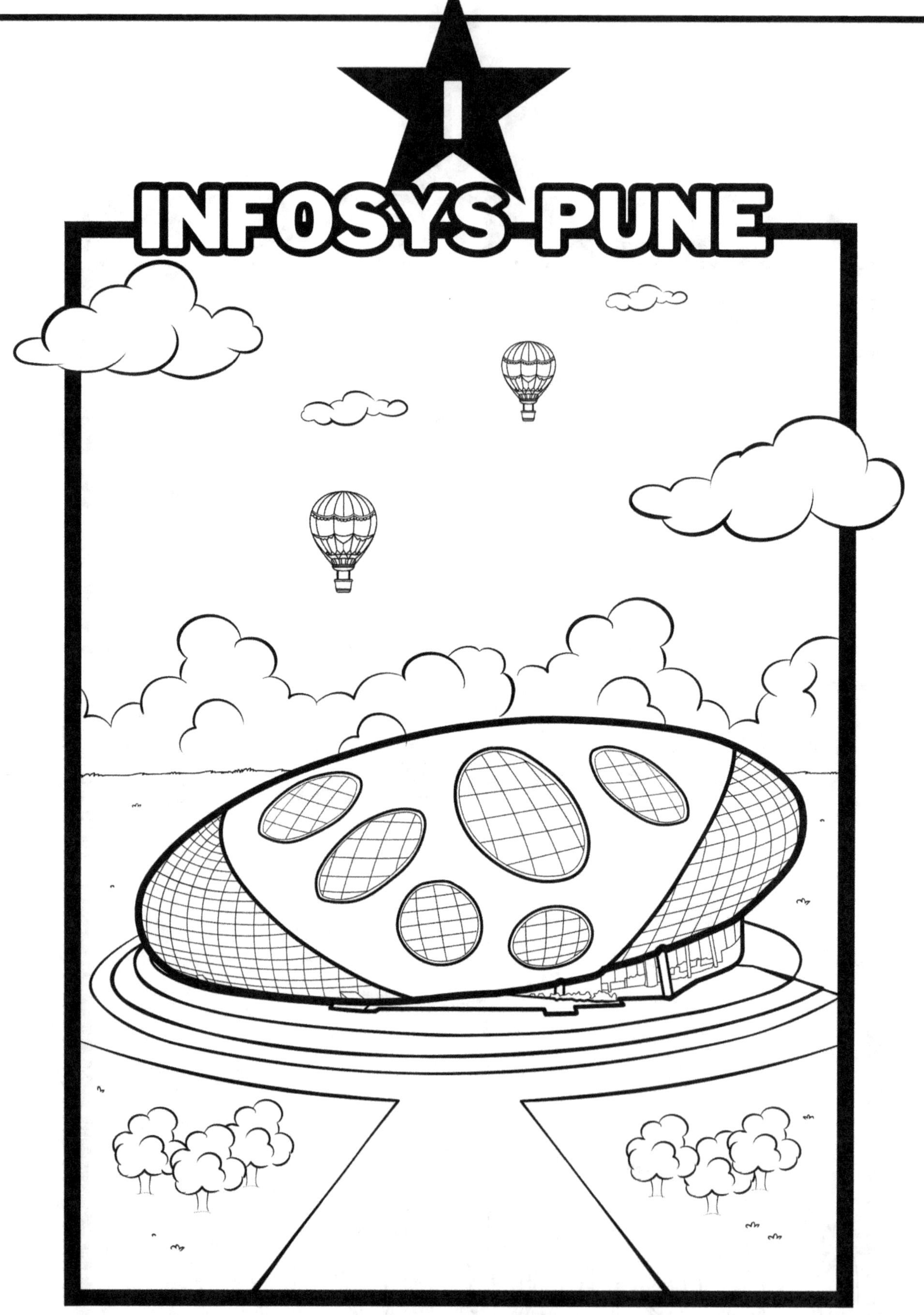

The Infosys Pune is a business headquarters in Pune, India. This building is part of a campus for the staff of the information technology company “Infosys”. The giant “spaceship” style futuristic building was designed by architect Hafeez Contractor and built in 2004.

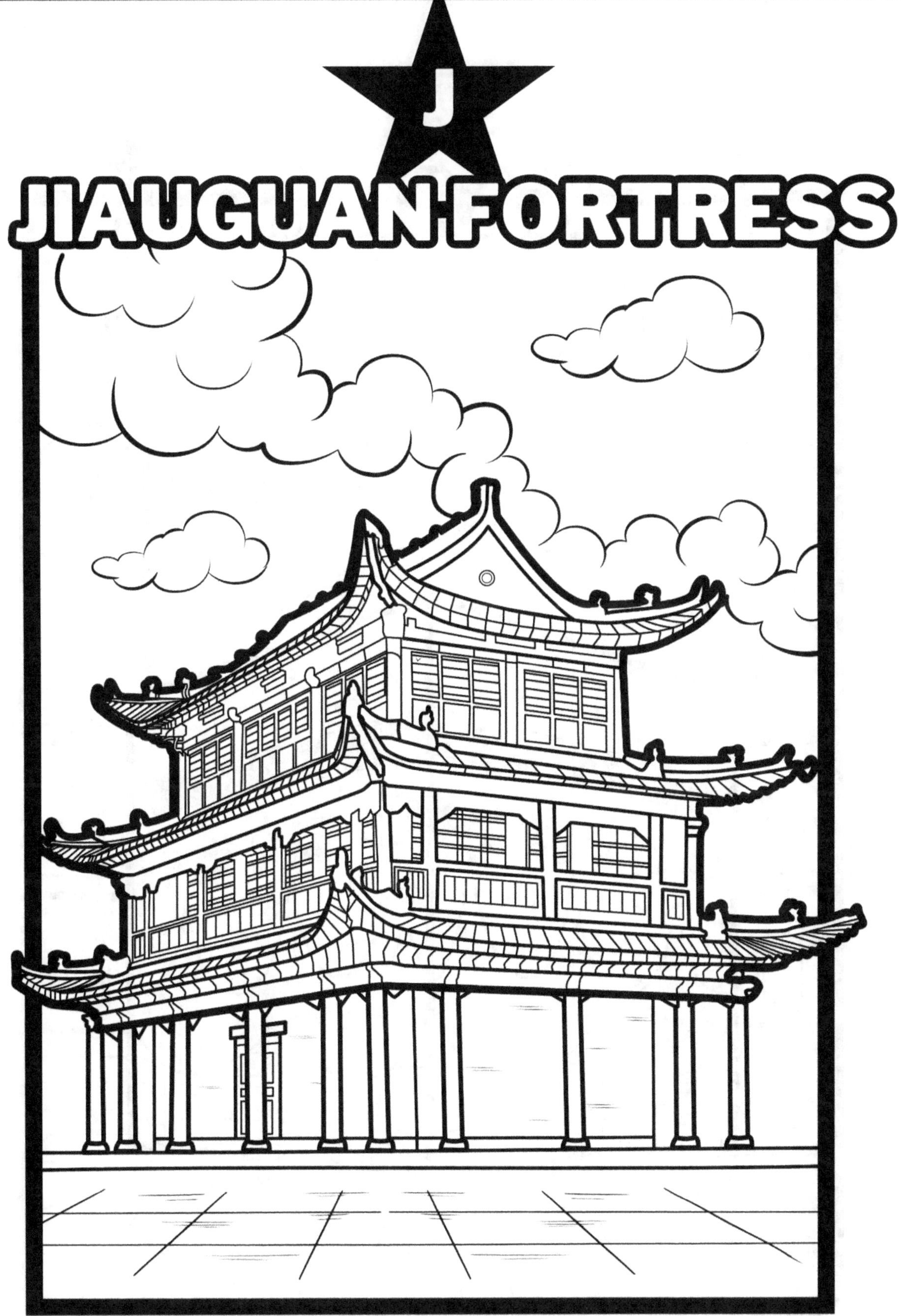

Jiauguan Fortress, also known as Jiayu Pass, is one of the main passes of the Great Wall of China. The design and construction were overseen by General Qi Jiguang during the Ming Dynasty of China in 1372.

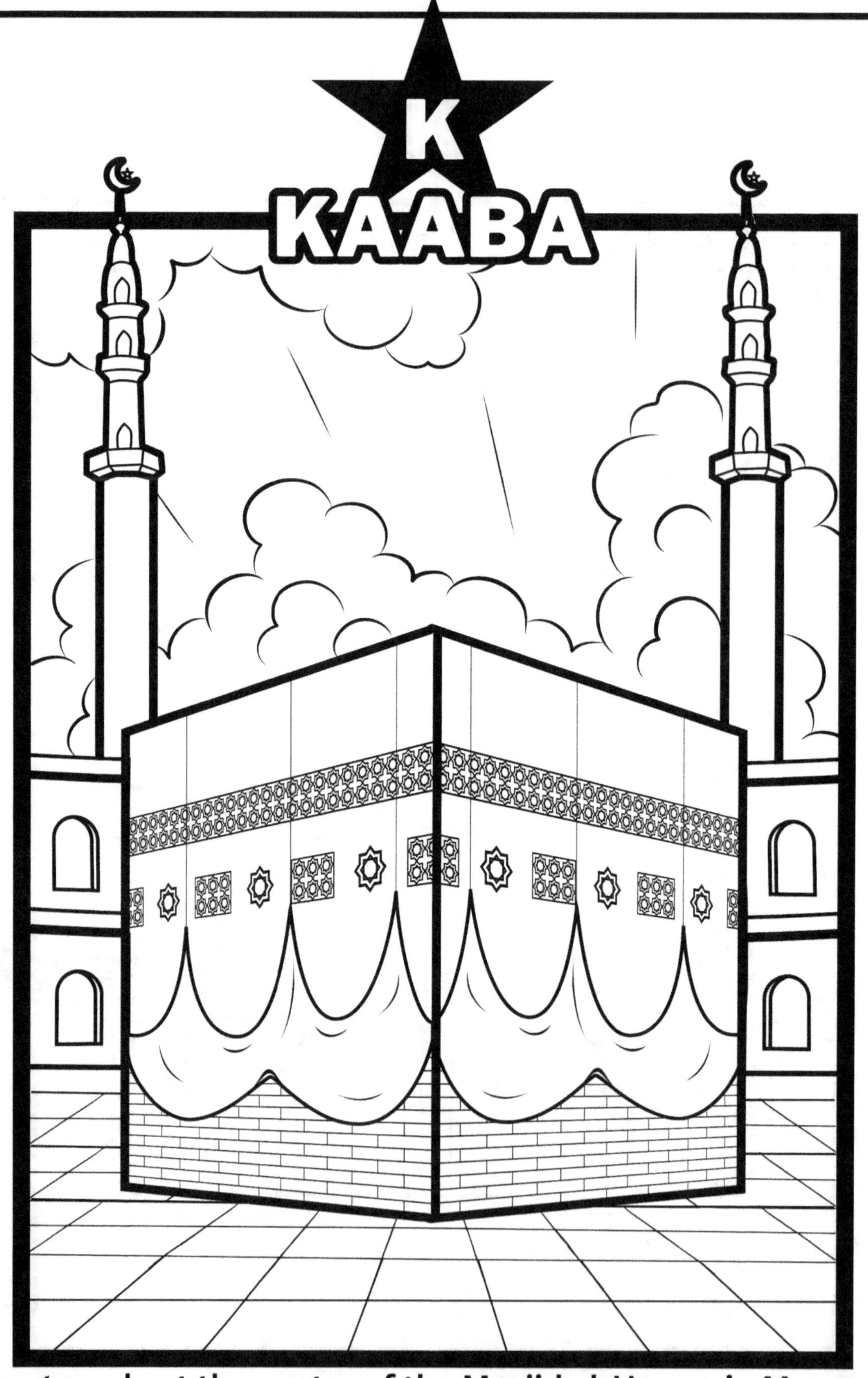

Kaaba is a temple at the center of the Masjid al-Haram in Mecca, Saudi Arabia. Muslims believe that Abraham and his son, Ismail, constructed the Kaaba. The Kaaba's construction date is not known, as it predates recorded history.

L

LEANING TOWER OF PISA

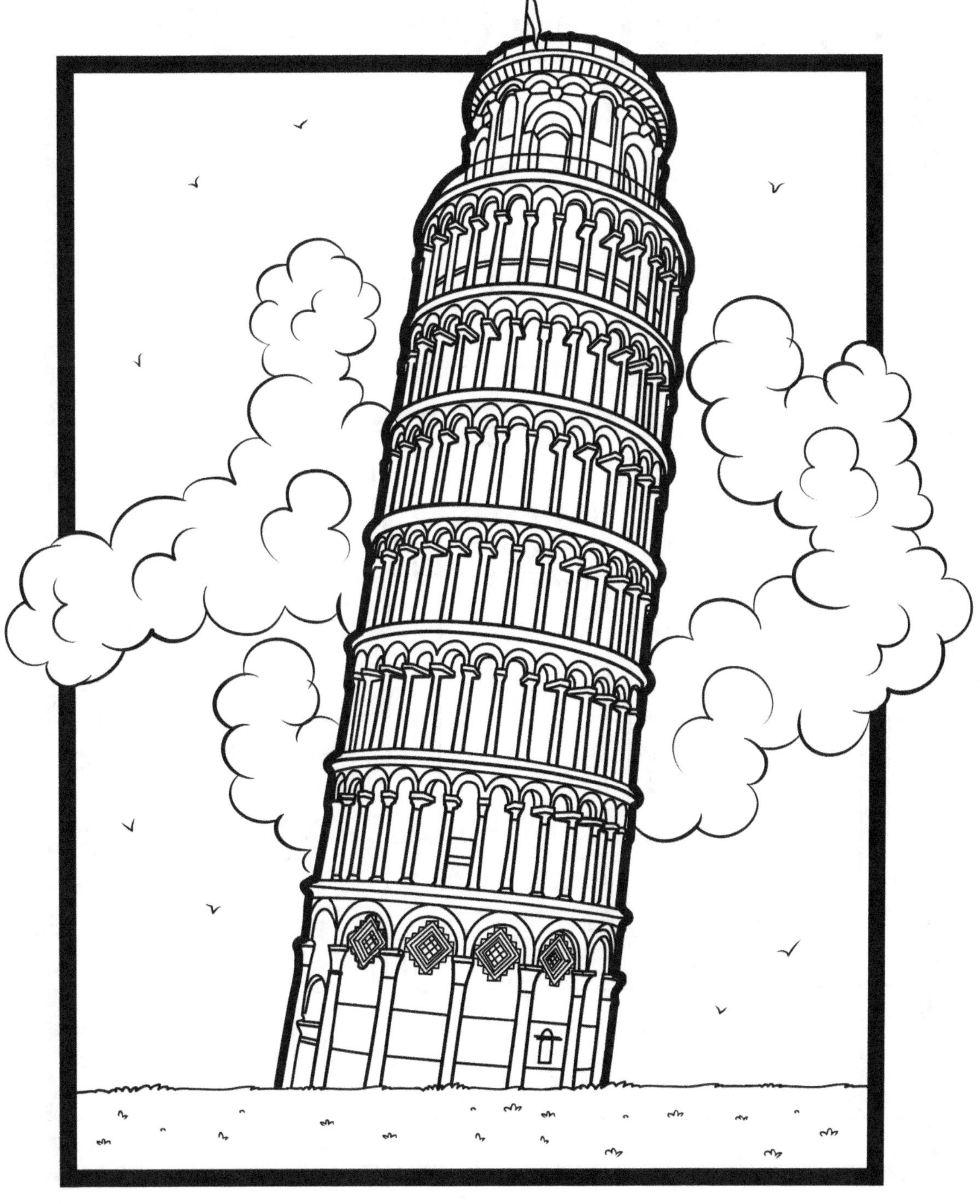

The Leaning Tower of Pisa is located in Rome, Italy and is known for its four-degree lean. It was completed in 1372. The tower's lean is the result of an unstable foundation. The identity of Tower of Pisa's architects is a mystery.

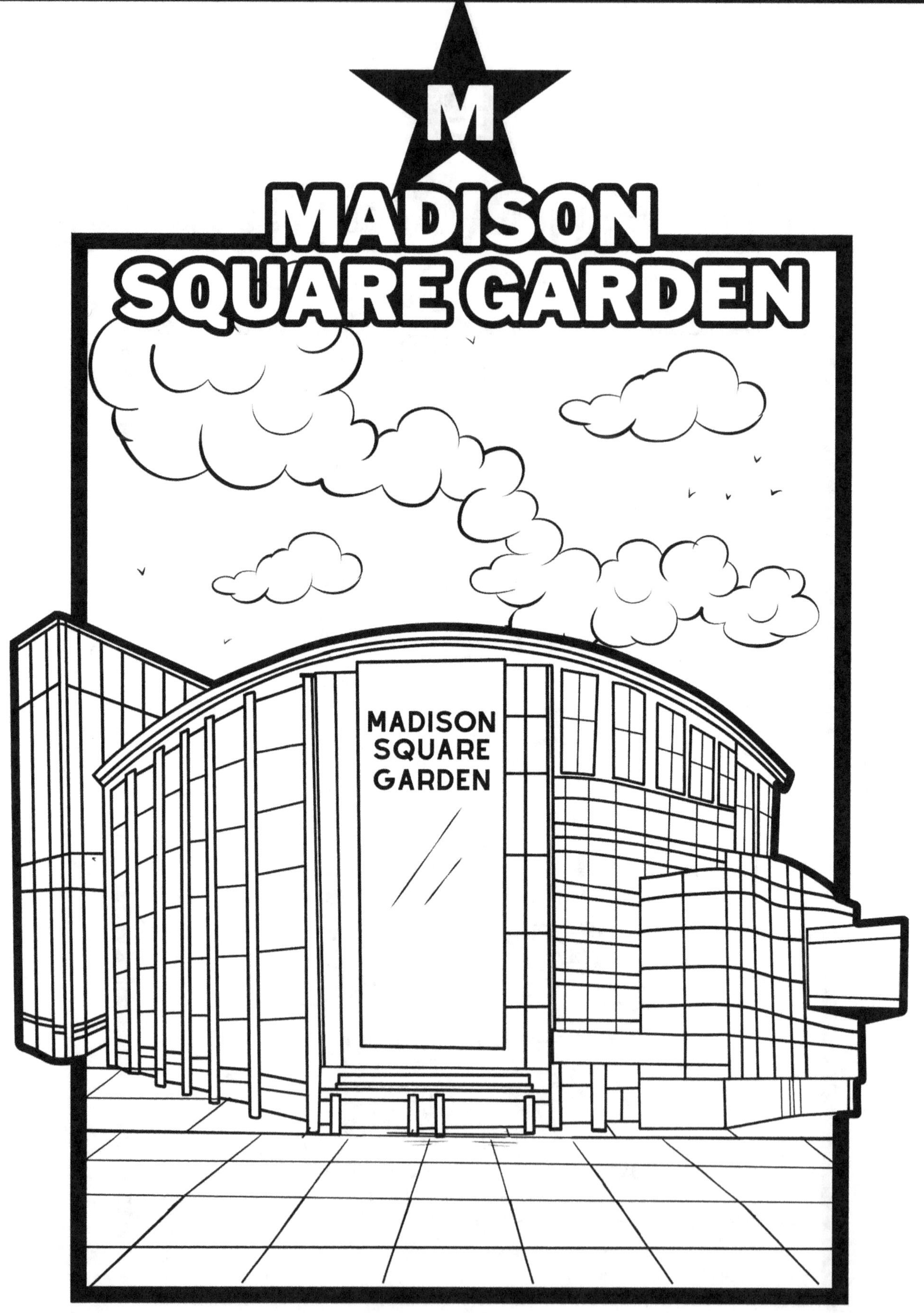

Madison Square Garden is a multi-purpose arena in New York City in the United States of America. The building has been renovated under the design of Architect Stanford White and opened on February 11, 1879.

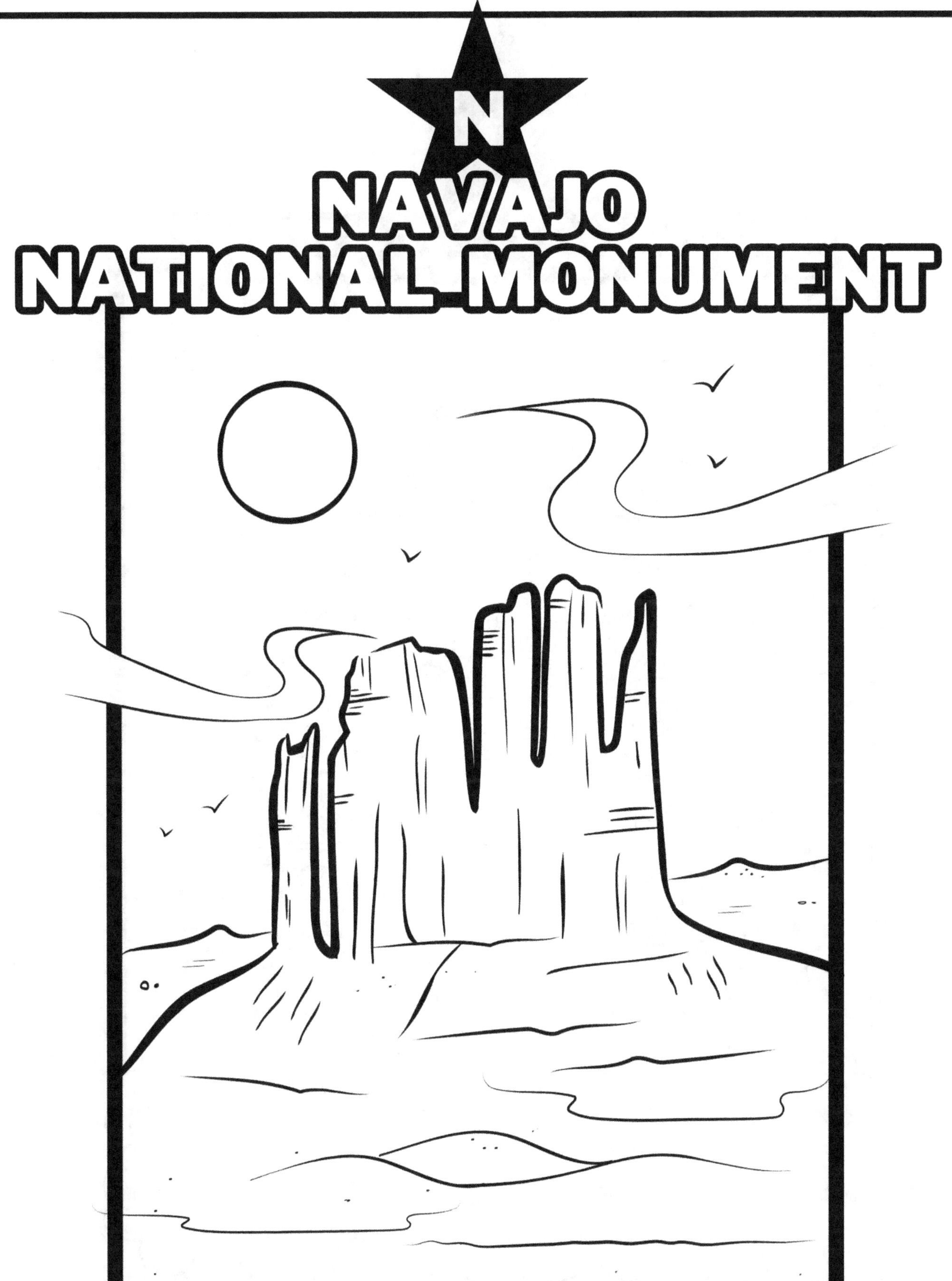

The Navajo National Monument consists of three cliff dwellings of ancestral Puebloan people. It is located in Arizona in the United States of America and the landmark was established by President William Howard Taft in 1909.

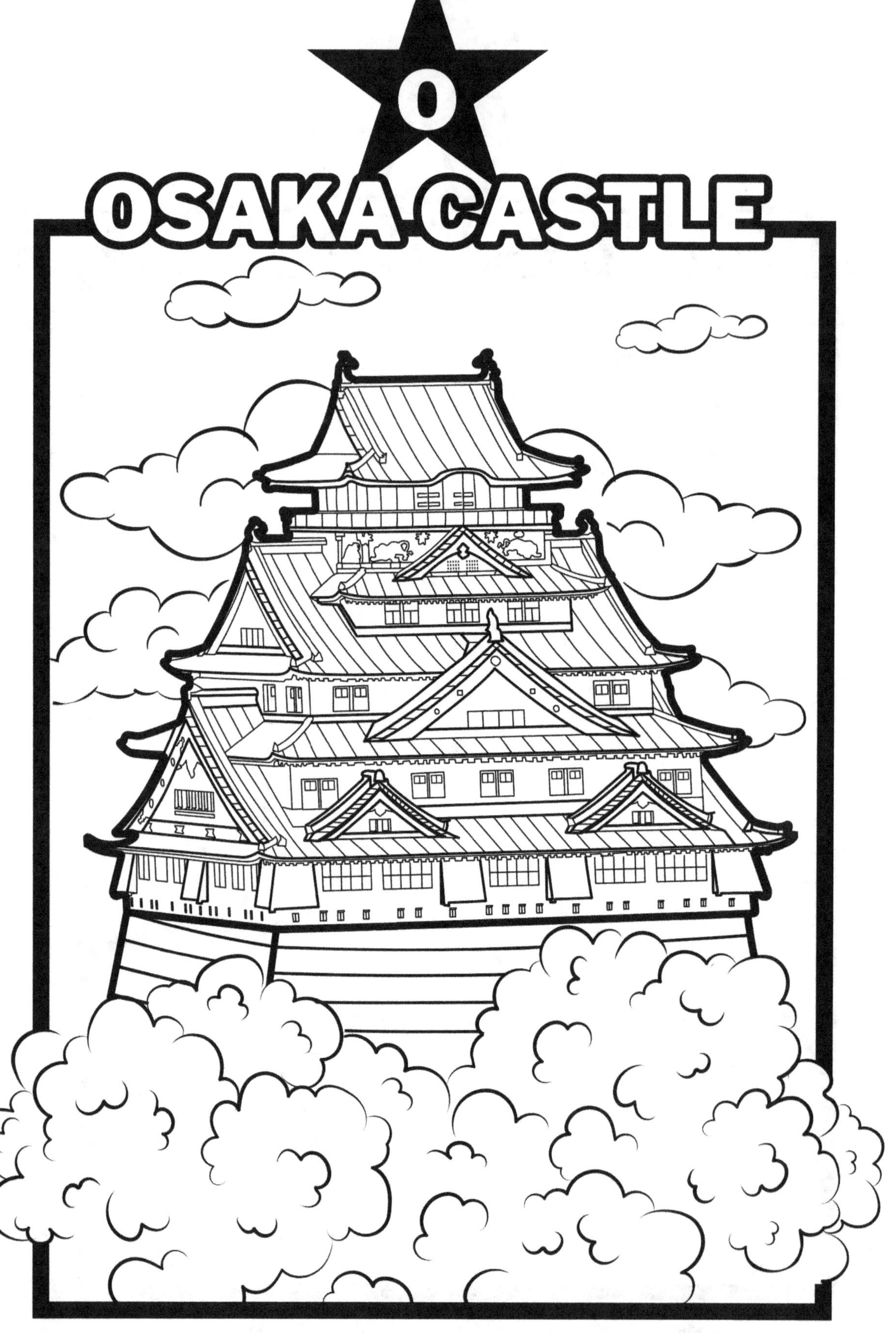

Osaka Castle is a Japanese castle in Chūō-ku, Osaka, Japan. Toyotomi Hideyoshi was the original designer of Osaka Castle in the late 16th century.

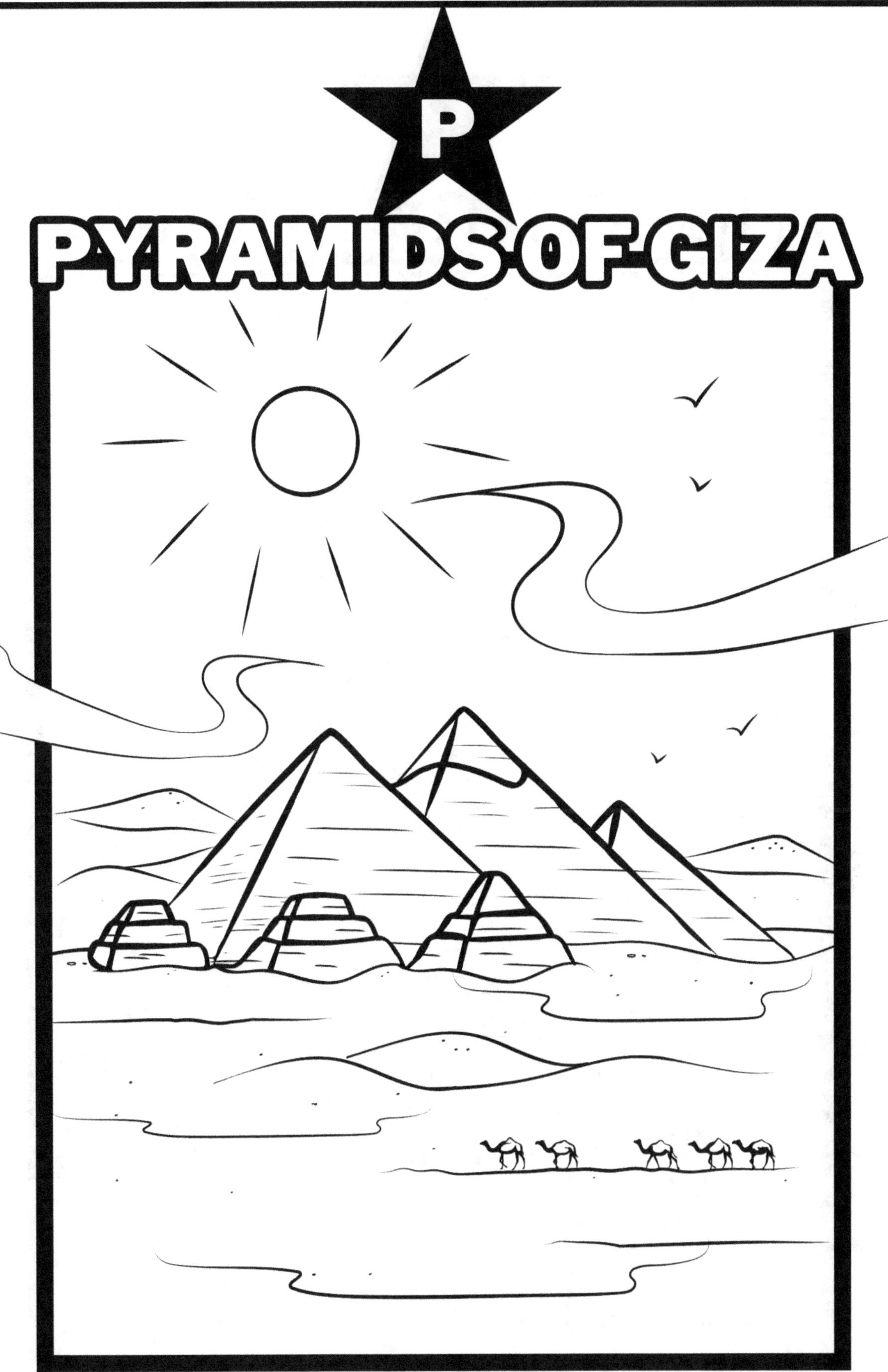

The Pyramids of Giza are three pyramids near the Nile River in Egypt.
The pyramids were built for Kings Khufu, Khafre, and Menkaure.
Their construction took place over several decades in the 26th century BCE.

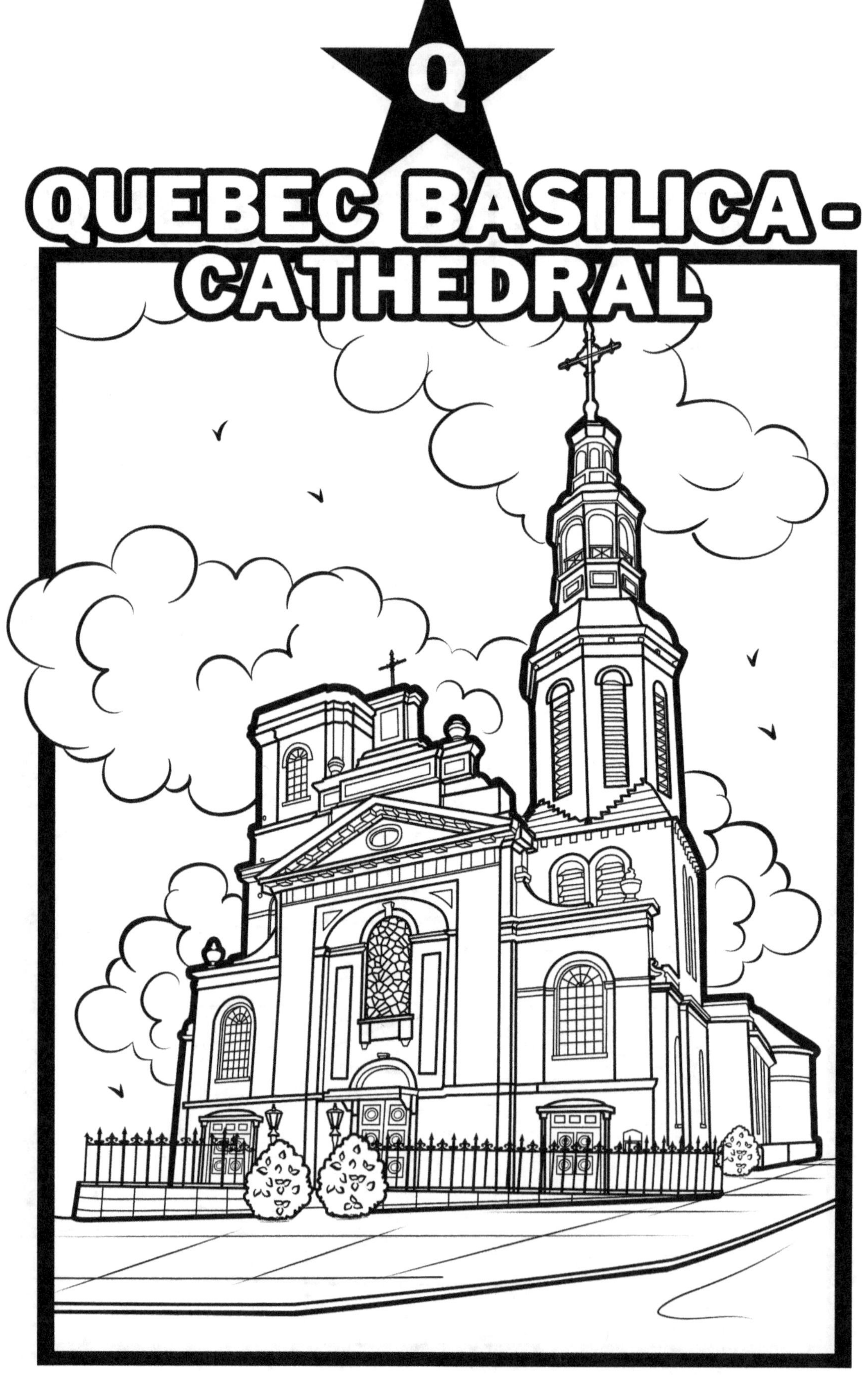

The Cathedral-Basilica of Notre-Dame de Québec is the oldest church in Canada. It is located in Québec, Canada, and was rebuilt from plans by Gaspard-Joseph Chaussegros de Léry in 1743 after a fire.

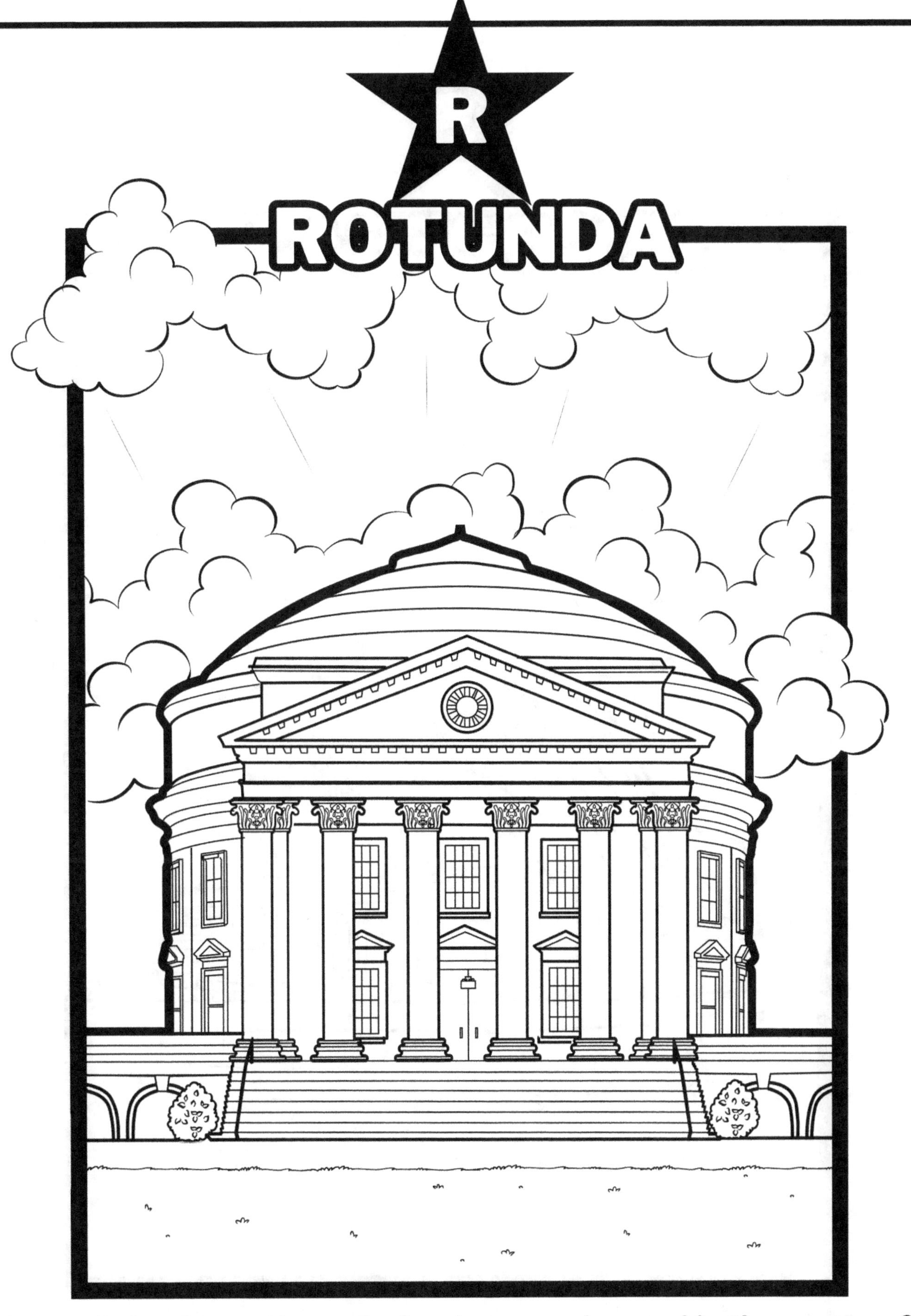

The Rotunda is a large, domed, circular room located in the center of the United States Capitol Building in Washington, D.C. President Thomas Jefferson designed the structure and construction began in 1822.

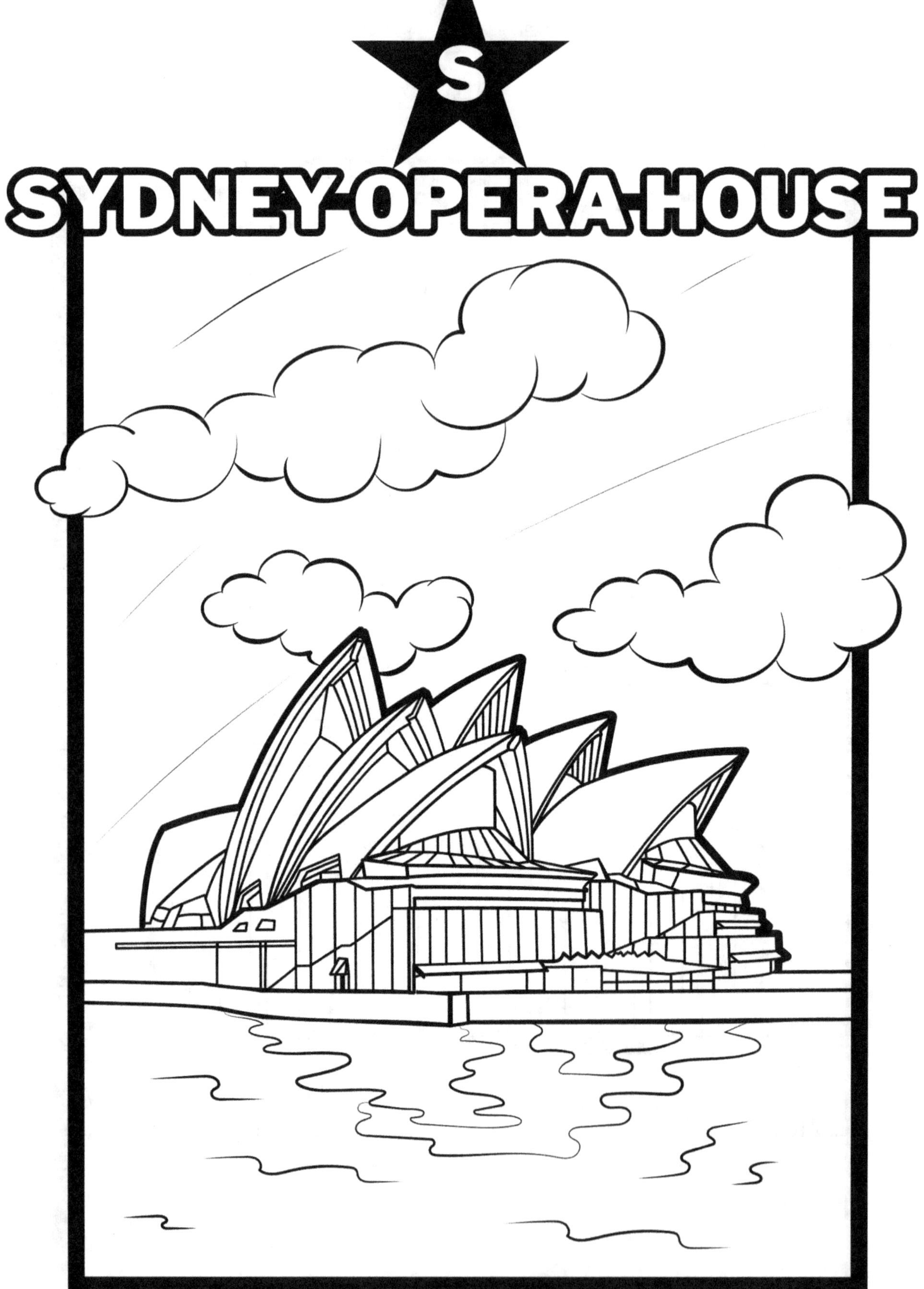

The Sydney Opera House is a multi-venue performing arts center located in Sydney, Australia. Sydney Opera House was designed by architect Jørn Utzon and construction began in 1959.

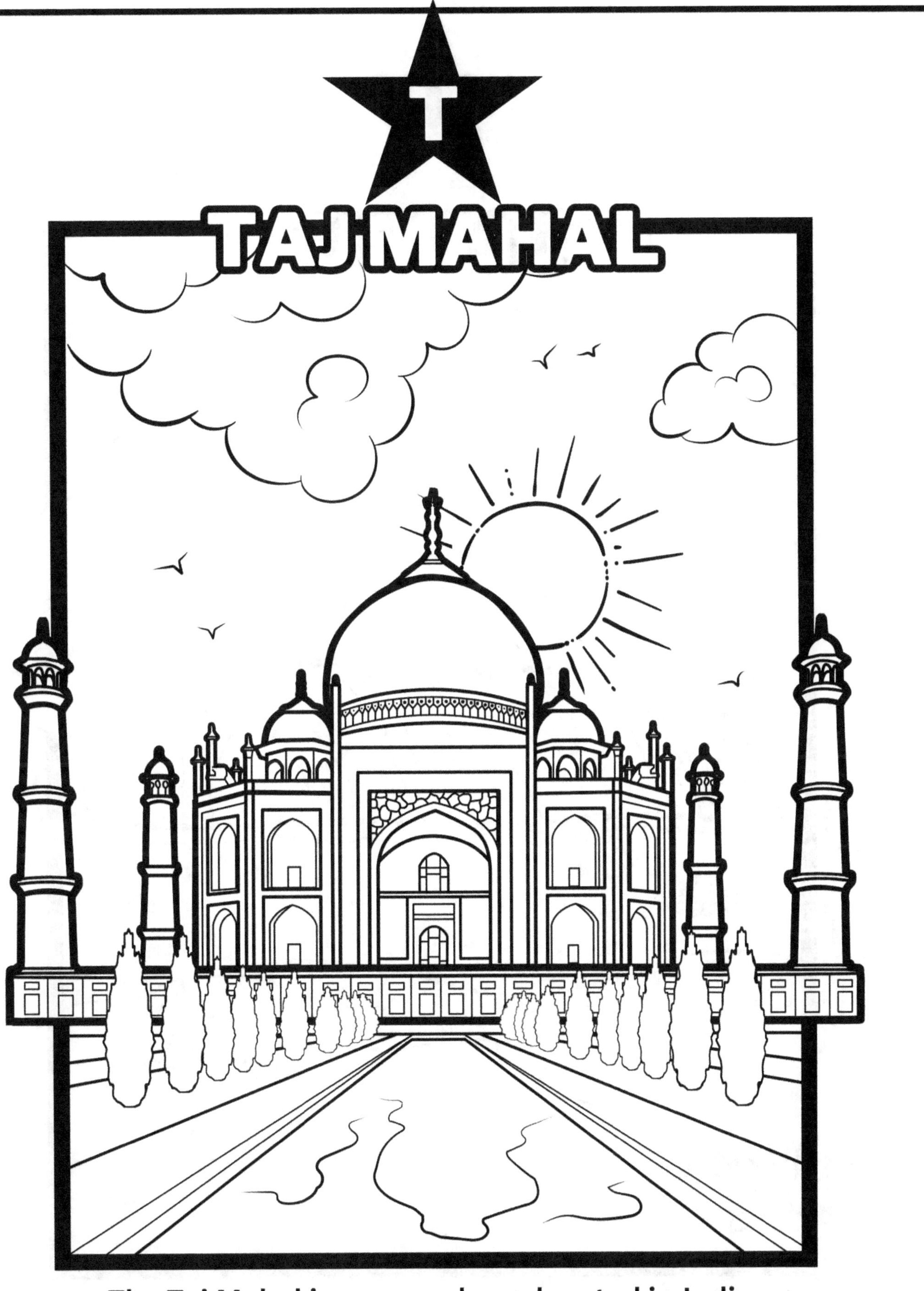

The Taj Mahal is a mausoleum located in India.
Emperor Shah Jahan had the building created to house the tomb of his wife, Mumtaz Mahal in 1632. The emperor's court architect was Ustad Lahori.

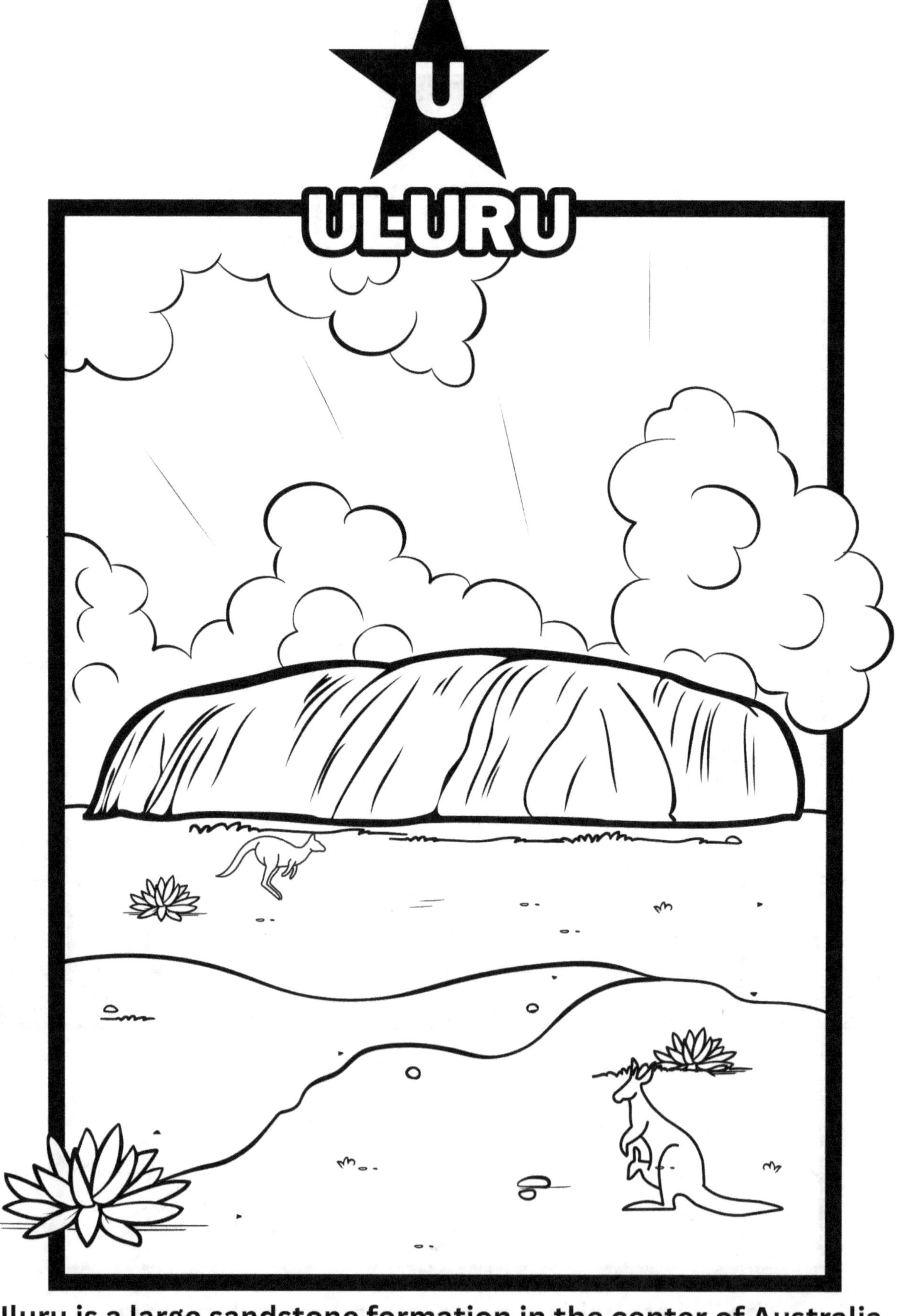

Uluru is a large sandstone formation in the center of Australia. It is also known as “Ayers Rock”. About 550 million years ago, hardened sandstone layers were uplifted to form the mountain.

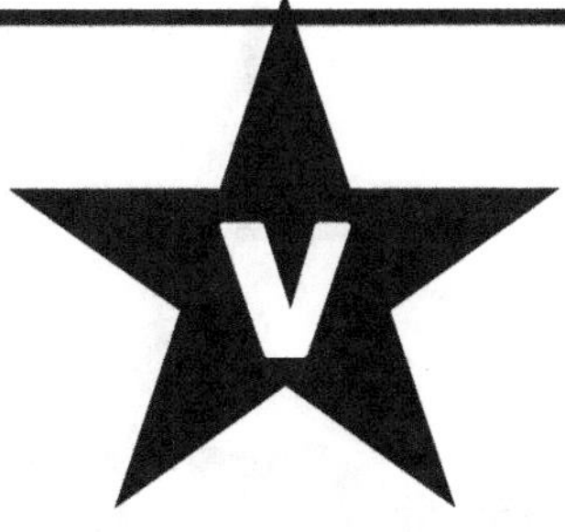

VILLA SAVOYE

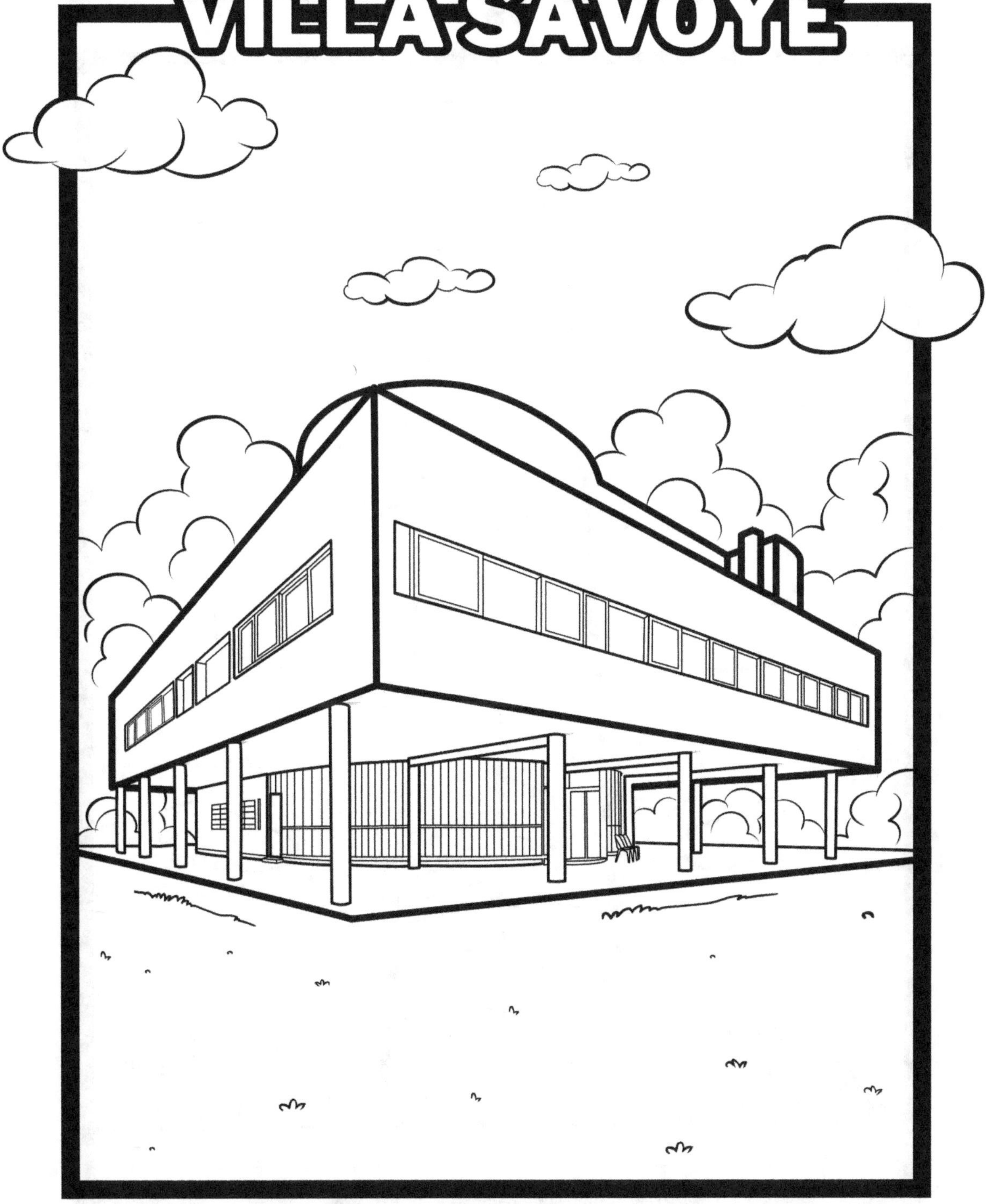

Villa Savoye is a modernist villa in Poissy, near Paris, France. It was designed by architect Le Corbusier and his cousin Pierre Jeanneret and built in 1928.

W

WASHINGTON MONUMENT

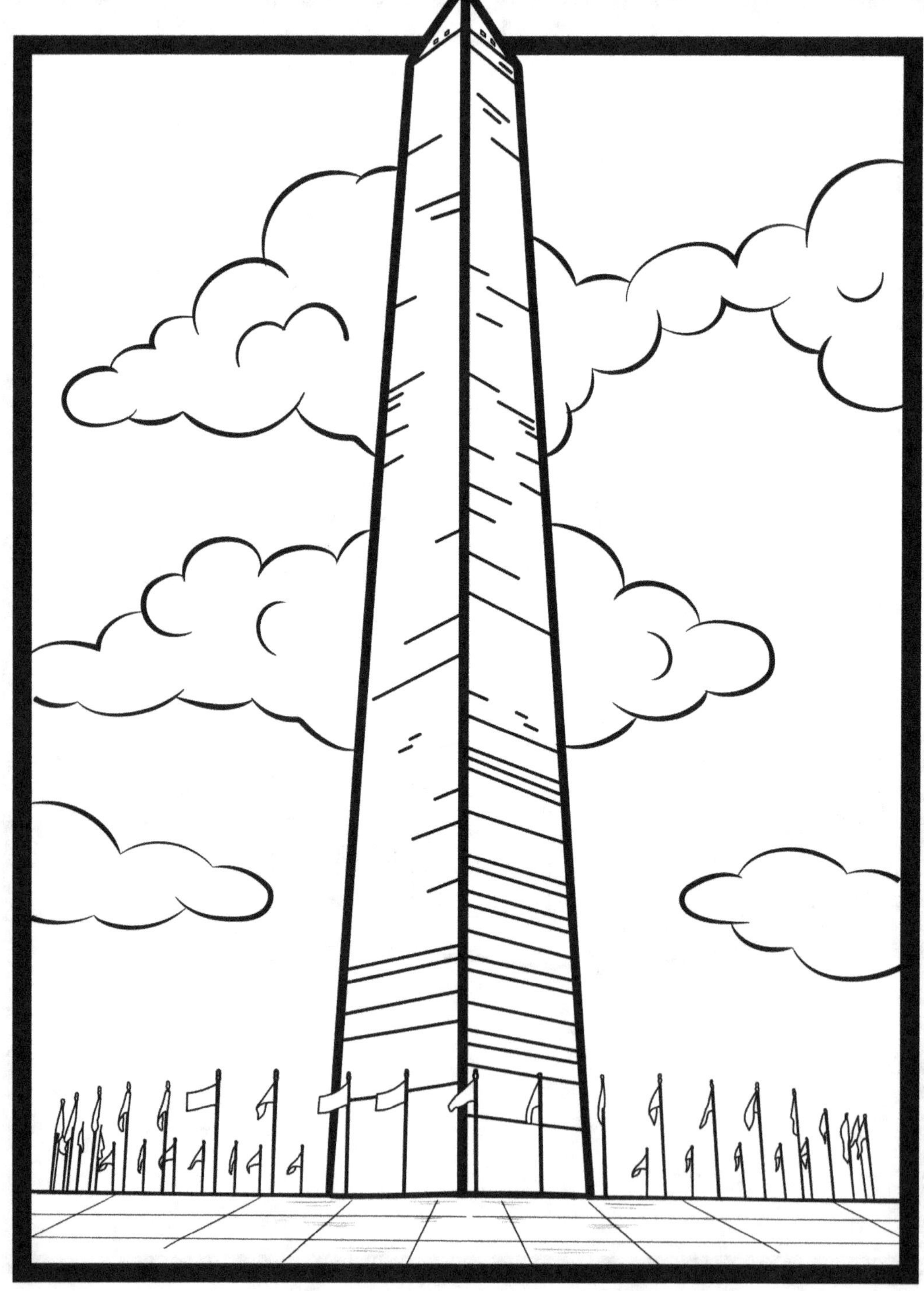

The Washington Monument is an obelisk in Washington, D.C., built to commemorate George Washington, a Founding Father of the United States. The original design was by Robert Mills in 1833.

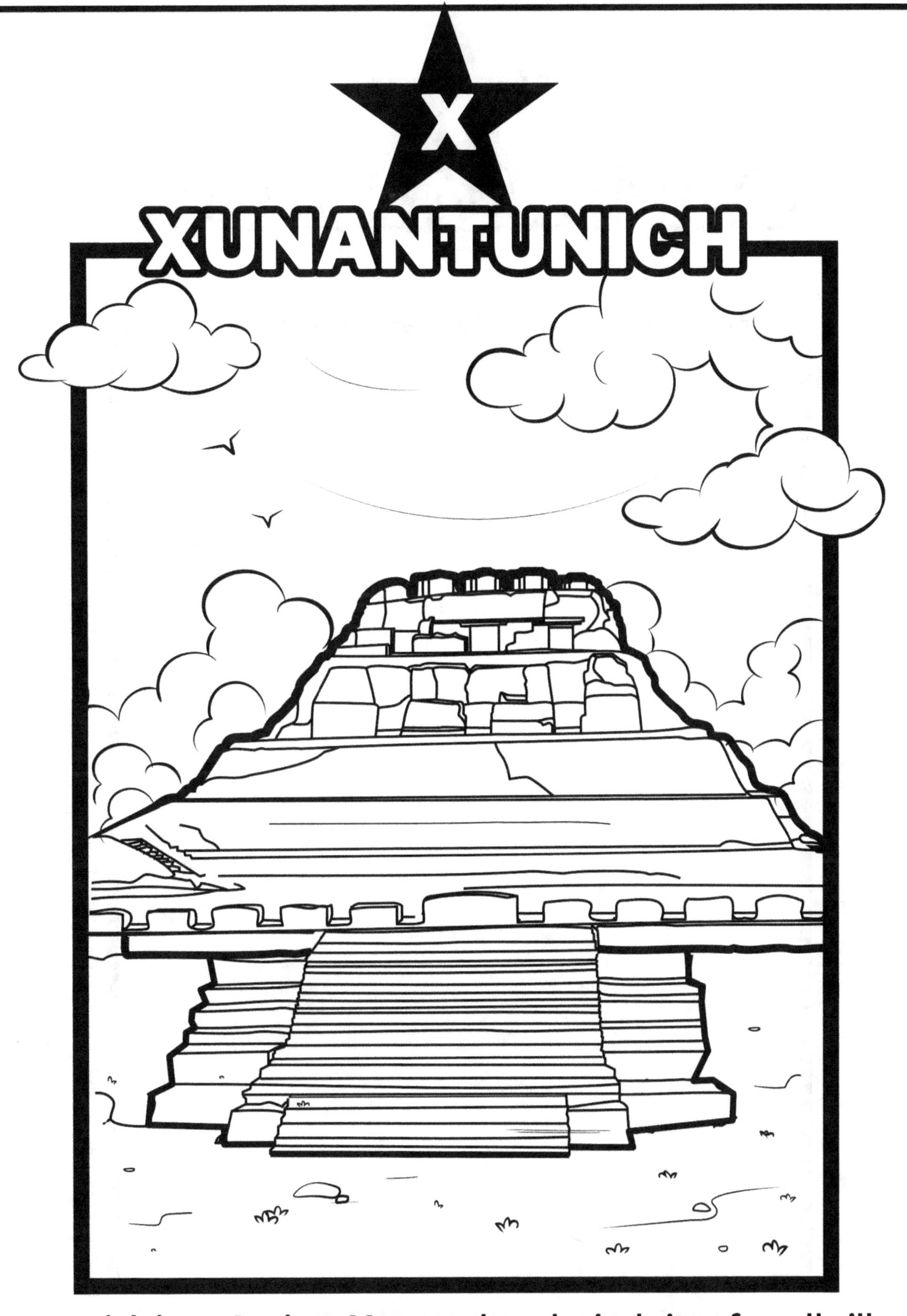

Xunantunich is an Ancient Maya archaeological site of small villages in Belize. Xunantunich's name means "Maiden of the Rock" in the Maya language. It is believed to have been founded between 1000 BC to 250 AD.

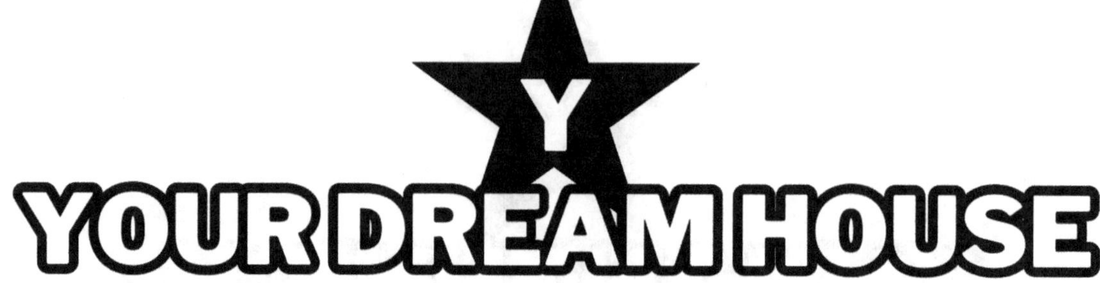

Imagine yourself being the architect of YOUR very own dream home!
What would your dream home look like?
Draw and color your dream house!

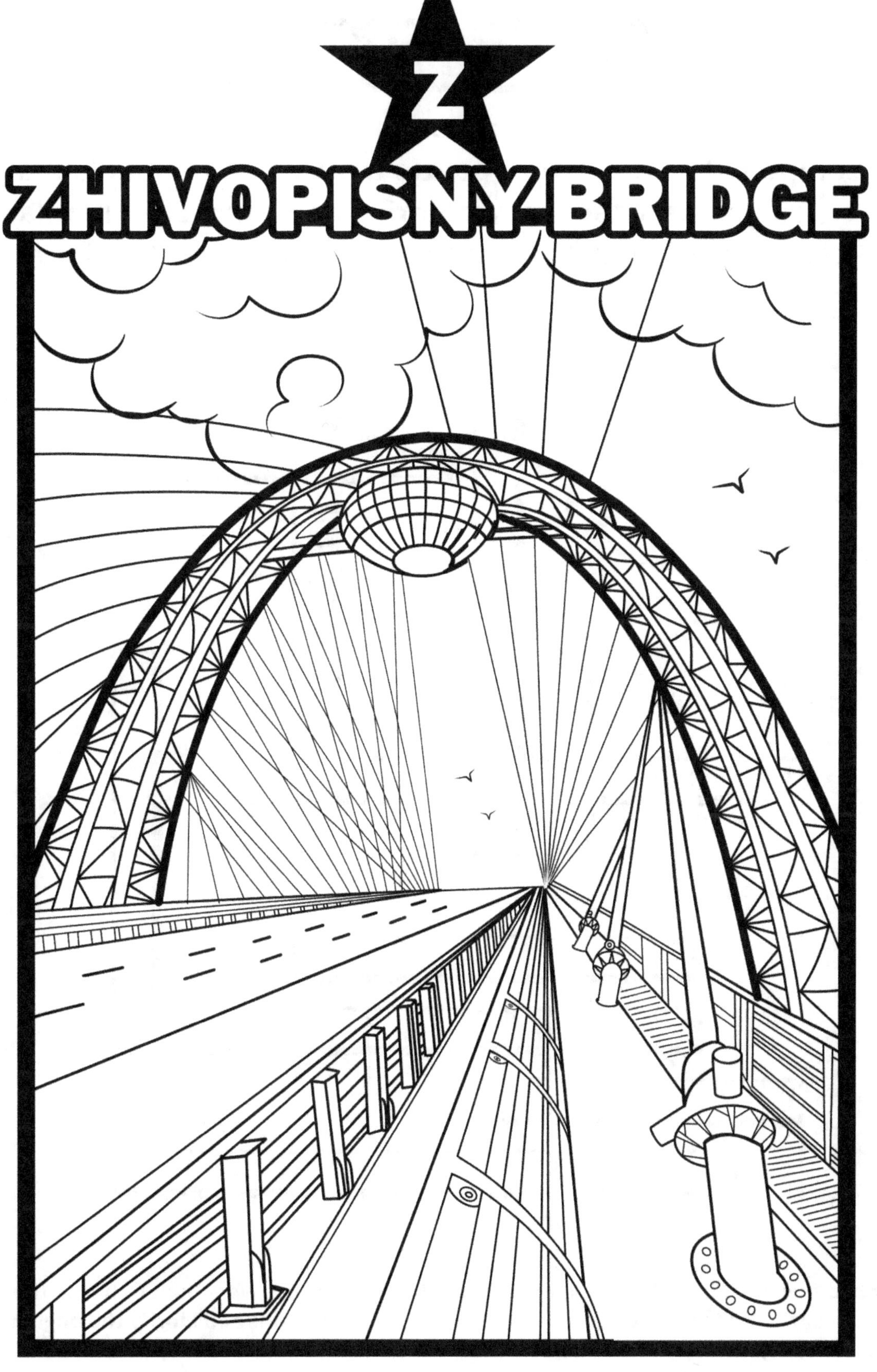

Zhivopisny Bridge is a cable-stayed bridge that spans the Moskva River in north-western Moscow, Russia. This bridge was designed by Architect Nikolay Shumakov and opened in 2007.

THE END!

Now that we've explored landmarks around the world, let's test your knowledge! Complete this crossword puzzle trivia game that includes a few of the landmarks listed in the coloring book and a few new landmarks! It is ok to ask for help from siblings, parents, or teachers!

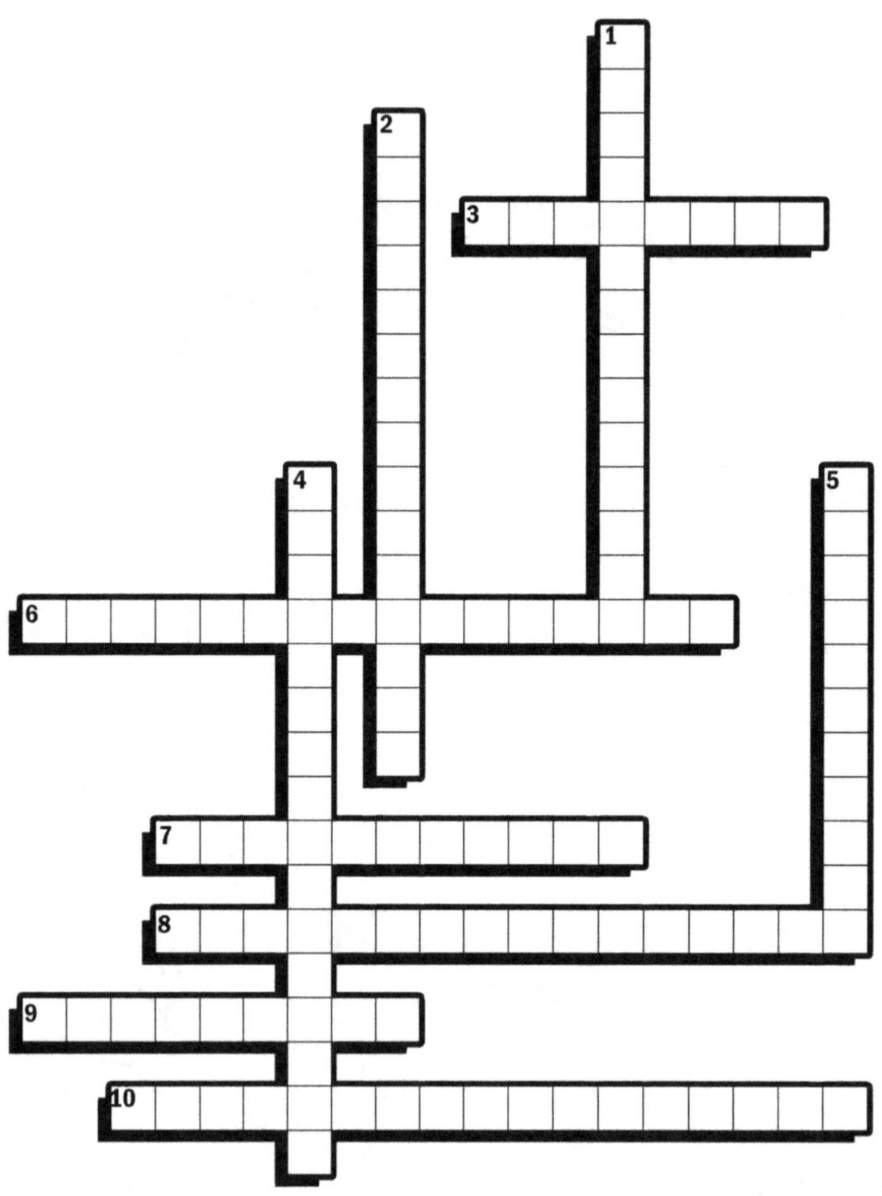

Across:

3. An emperor had this building built in memory of his wife
6. The "birthplace of the United States"
7. This building is leaning at a four-degree angle
8. You can use a toboggan and slide down the side of this monument in two minutes
9. The southernmost point on earth. It is situated on the continent of Antarctica
10. A giant statue of Jesus Christ in Brazil on the continent of South Africa

Down:

1. These were built to house the tombs of pharaohs and glorify the beginning of a journey to the other world in the afterlife
2. A gift to the United States from Paris
4. This building's roof is made of a series of gleaming white sail-shaped shells
5. The world's tallest building

www.ingramcontent.com/pod-product-compliance
Lightning Source LLC
LaVergne TN
LVHW061258100826
845148LV00008B/1172

* 9 7 9 8 2 1 8 3 2 7 0 1 9 *